What to Do
WHEN YOU
DON'T KNOW
What to Do

Dr. Henry Cloud
Dr. John Townsend

THOMAS NELSON
Since 1798

NASHVILLE DALLAS MEXICO CITY RIO DE JANEIRO

Published in Nashville, Tennessee, by Thomas Nelson®. Thomas Nelson® is a registered trademark of Thomas Nelson, Inc.

Published in association with Yates & Yates, LLP, Literary Agents, Orange, California.

Thomas Nelson, Inc. titles may be purchased in bulk for educational, business, fund-raising, or sales promotional use. For information, please e-mail SpecialMarkets@ThomasNelson.com.

Unless otherwise noted, all Scripture references are from *The Holy Bible*, NEW KING JAMES VERSION. All rights reserved. © 1982 by Thomas Nelson, Inc.

Scripture references marked niv are taken from the HOLY BIBLE, NEW INTERNATIONAL VERSION®. Copyright © 1973, 1978, 1984 International Bible Society. Used by permission of Zondervan Publishing House. All rights reserved.

Scripture references marked nLt are taken from the *Holy Bible*, New Living Translation © 1996. Used by permission of Tyndale House Publishers, Inc., Wheaton, Ill. All rights reserved.

Cover design by Anderson Thomas Design, Nashville, TN

ISBN-13: 978-1-4041-8773-3

Printed and bound in China

09 10 11 12 [WC] 5 4 3 2 1

www.thomasnelson.com

CONTENTS

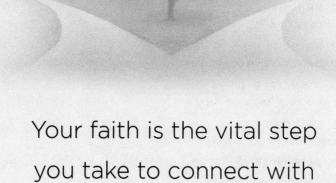

Your faith is the vital step
you take to connect with
God, the way-maker.

God Will Make a Way

Recently on our national radio talk show we received a call from Marian, a middle-class career woman who was on the verge of losing it all, even her husband and children. In a not-so-smart moment, she had "just once" tried crack cocaine. Drug use was totally out of character for this respected Midwestern mother, but because of the power of chemical addiction, she was not able to do cocaine "just once." The drug had instantly gripped her, and she suddenly found herself to be something that she never would have imagined—an addict. She had no idea what to do or where to turn.

Helpless, hopeless, and feeling terribly guilty, Marian turned to God. She made a commitment to being good, mustered up her will to stop the drug use, and began attending church. But doing the "God thing" was not working. Nothing was changing. Now believing that not even God would help her, she was more desperate than before.

Marian was not finding God; she was only finding religion. Big difference. Religion is about trying to be better and using "God language" to do it. If she had found God, she would have found help and strength beyond her own efforts. Instead, she seemed like a half-dead person trying to shock herself back to life with electric paddles.

God's way, we explained, does not depend on our willpower to transform a hopeless situation. He can raise people from the dead and create life where none exists. We said we wanted to see her in a program, surrounded by other addicts through whom God could provide his help and express his love and support. We asked Marian to abandon her effort to help herself by sheer human willpower and to reach out for God to meet her where she was. And we prayed for God to do a miracle for her.

Marian was willing to do all we suggested. She opened herself to God's help, and that's when the miracle began. Here's how it happened: We knew just the drug rehabilitation center she needed, but she didn't have the money to pay for it and had no idea how to get it. So we prayed that God would make a way.

Within minutes, the phone began ringing. People from all over the country called to say they felt God moving them to help pay for Marian's treatment. Money was pouring in, and we were certain that God had answered our prayer. But at the end of the program we were dismayed to find that we had come up short—$5,400 short, to be exact. But God was not through yet. The phone rang again, and a woman told us that she had received an inheritance and felt God moving her to give a gift for this woman's treatment.

"How much is your gift?" we asked.

"The inheritance was $54,000," she replied. "I want to give ten percent—$5,400."

We were ecstatic! God had indeed made a way. Within a short time Marian was in treatment and, as of this writing, she is doing great.

Little did Marian know that her call from the Midwest to a radio studio in California would land her in a treatment center in Arizona, paid for by people from several other states. Stories like Marian's tell us that God shows up in many ways and changes even the most hopeless situations. One of the most powerful lessons we can learn is that even when bad things happen and we don't know what to do about them, we can trust God to be present and working on our behalf, creating a path through the most painful wilderness. Even when the problem is of our own making.

The main obstacle to following God's way through crises is failing to trust him. Most of us have little difficulty believing in God. But for some reason we balk when it comes to really trusting God. Our doubts rage like a rising river: *Will he come through for me? Can I depend on him?*

Trust is the bridge over that river. The way God makes for you means nothing until you step on the bridge and start walking. Trust is both an attitude and an action. You must follow your first small step with another and another. The more you act on your faith in God, the more you will see of his way for you.

God is active on your behalf, even when you cannot see it. Faith calls you to be active also. This may seem like a paradox. Am I doing it? Or is God doing it? The answer to both questions is yes. God will do what only he can do, and your job is to do what you can do. Marian could not kick her crack habit or find the money for treatment. God had to do all of that. She did not know what to do, but she acted by praying to him to do something, and by taking the steps he placed before her. That's faith.

The God who made a way for Marian is available to you now. He watches over all of the earth, with an ear attuned to all who desire him. As the psalmist said, "The LORD is near to all who call upon Him, to all who call upon Him in truth. He will fulfill the desire of those who fear Him; He also will hear their cry and save them" (Psalm 145:18–19).

God wired us to
depend on Him.

Begin Your Journey with God

I t almost sounds like some kind of advertising slogan, but this little play on words really says it: "God will make a way" begins with God. It's not your belief that makes a way; it's God who makes a way. Your faith is the vital step you take to connect with God, the way-maker. But without God, all the faith you can possibly muster won't get you anywhere. *So our first principle for finding God's way is to begin your journey with God.*

The story of Abraham in the Bible is a good example. When God called him to leave his homeland, Abraham had no idea where he was headed. But he believed God knew where he was headed, so he packed up and left. He did not believe in belief; he believed in a God who knew exactly where Abraham was going and who was able to lead him there.

So when we talk about faith, trust, and belief to carry you through your trials and troubles, we mean it in a very specific way. We're not talking about warm religious feelings or an exercise in positive thinking. Faith is grounded in a relationship with God, a real Person who knows the way for you and promises to lead you on it.

We Are Designed for Dependence

Some people argue that relying on God is a weakness, that God is a crutch for those who can't make it on their own. The fact that you need God so desperately in your life is not a weakness any more than your need for air or for food is a weakness. God created us to reach outside ourselves to find the things we need. We were designed for dependence on him. The term "self-made person" is a huge oxymoron. No one is self-made. The psalmist writes, "It is [God] who has made us, and not we ourselves; we are His people and the sheep of His pasture" (Psalm 100:3).

We did not create ourselves to begin with, nor were we designed to find our own way in life. Rather, God wired us to depend on him. When you exercise faith in him, you are doing the one thing you can do to accomplish superhuman feats: You are reaching beyond your own human strength and knowledge and tapping into God's infinite strength and knowledge.

God Provides What You Need

What do you do in a difficult or painful situation when you don't know what to do? The sad truth is that many people do one of two things. First, they repeat what didn't work before. They try harder to make a relationship work, to succeed in a career, or to overcome a difficult personal problem, pattern, or habit. Chronic dieters, for example, convince themselves that "this time it will work." The victim in an abusive relationship reconciles after another fight or separation, thinking this time the partner will change.

> God's resources are available to you.

This approach reflects a popular definition of insanity: *Doing the same thing again, but expecting different results.* If you have done everything you know to do without success, trying again with your own limited knowledge and strength is not the answer.

The second common response to a hopeless situation is to stop trying all together. These people just give up, believing the relationship will never work, they will never lose weight, they will never get over their depression, etc. Trying to get through life on your own limited strength, knowledge, and resources leads to futility and a loss of hope.

But in God's economy, getting to the end of yourself

is the beginning of hope. As Jesus said, "God blesses those who are poor and realize their need for him" (Matthew 5:3 NLT). When you realize that you are poor and helpless without God, you are ready to ask him for help. And the moment you ask God for help, you transcend your own limitations in finding your way, and God's resources are available to you.

No matter what limitation or circumstance you are struggling against, God can empower and equip you to go beyond what you thought possible. He can get you through a painful or tragic event, help you deal with a difficult relationship, and even make a long-held dream come true. Whatever it is, God will make a way for you, perhaps in very unexpected ways. And he does his best work when you are at the end of yourself—and you admit it.

Our "Yes" Is All God Needs

How does this miracle happen? What must we do to get past our own abilities and tap into the power, wisdom, and resources of God himself? It seems too good to be true. Is it only for really special, really good, or really unique people?

The Bible promises—and millions of people have discovered—that God's power and resources are equally available to everyone. They cannot be earned; they can only be received as a gift when we, in humility, acknowledge our need of our Creator. Throughout the Bible, God says repeatedly, "Come to me and I will provide what you need."

He's ready to get totally involved in your life. All you have to do is say yes to him. When you do, he will provide what you need to find the way.

Once on your journey with God, however, sometimes his way will be truly miraculous and sometimes it will involve a lot of work, growth, and change on your part. Sometimes it won't be the way you thought you needed, but a different and even better one. But when God makes a way, it is real, meaningful, and enduring.

Your journey with God is not intended to be a solo flight. In the next chapter we will explore God's choice for your traveling companions.

Your journey with God will
be richer, more fulfilling,
and more successful if you
surround yourself with
people who are committed
to support you.

Choose Your Traveling Companions Wisely

(Henry) grew up playing competitive golf, and when I was a youngster Jack Nicklaus was king of the sport. "The Golden Bear," as he is called, dominated the PGA tour for a number of years. From my vantage point, he was as close to being a god as a human could get.

Then one day my view of Jack Nicklaus abruptly changed. I heard that he would periodically travel home to Ohio to see his teacher, Jack Grout. Nicklaus needed some help with his swing, the announcer said. I was stunned. *Jack Nicklaus, the reigning god of professional golf, still needs a teacher? Jack is the best. Why does he need a teacher? I thought. Who could teach him anyway, since no one is better?*

In a kid-sized view of life, I assumed that if you were very good at something, the last thing you needed was a teacher. Teachers were for people who didn't know what they were doing. I have learned a lot since then. People who rise to become the best they can be in their sports or professions usually don't get to the top alone. They seek help from a teacher, a counselor, or a spiritual advisor.

This story illustrates our second principle for finding God's way. *Your journey with God will be richer, more fulfilling, and more successful if you surround yourself with people who are committed to support you, encourage you, assist you and pray for you.*

Part of God's program to make a way for you is to put good people around you who are gifted in helping you get where you need to go. Some of these people will just show up in your life, sent by God at just the right time. Others you will have to seek out on your own. Some will be professionals. Others may just be a neighbor or friend at church. Here are some important qualities and characteristics to look for in people as you select your traveling companions for the journey.

SUPPORT. Whenever you are negotiating a change in your life, solving a problem, or trying to reach a goal, you are pushing uphill. Such effort takes more energy than normal day-to-day living, and it can quickly drain you of emotional, physical, and spiritual strength. Notice the people who come around during these times ready to help. Someone may call to ask, "Is there anything I can do for you?" Someone may show up at your door to help you with a chore. Someone may e-mail you to say, "I'm praying for you." You need people around you who will help you shoulder the load in different ways.

> Your system of values will guide you as you follow God's way.

LOVE. The Bible says, "Above all, love each other deeply, because love covers over a multitude of sins"

(1 Peter 4:8 NIV). No matter what has happened to you, what you have done, or what you must do, you need the safety net of love. You need people on your team who love you deeply just as you are, faults included. Love helps take the sting out of life and makes it possible for you to do what you have to do.

COURAGE. You cannot journey God's way without encountering risk and fear. Sometimes the task looks too daunting to face. There is safety in numbers, so just having a support team close by will build your courage. But you also need people nearby who will tell you what Paul told his friends who were in great danger: "So keep up your courage, men, for I have faith in God that it will happen just as he told me" (Acts 27:25 NIV).

FEEDBACK. You need honest feedback from people if you hope to get where you're going in life. We're talking about people who are not afraid to correct you when you are wrong. Wise King Solomon wrote, "Like an earring of gold or an ornament of fine gold is a wise man's rebuke to a listening ear" (Proverbs 25:12 NIV).

WISDOM. You do not have all the wisdom and knowledge you need to make it through life. God has deposited some of it in other people. Keep your eye out for wise people through whom God will speak to you and direct you.

EXPERIENCE. How valuable and helpful it is to have someone on your team who has been where you are and understands what you are going through. In times of trouble or growth, seek out the experience of others who have traveled this road before you.

MODELING. It is difficult to do what we have never seen someone else do. One of God's greatest gifts for the journey is people who can serve as role models for us to follow. As Hebrews puts it: "We do not want you to become lazy, but to imitate those who through faith and patience inherit what has been promised" (6:12 NIV). Study and learn from people who are doing what you want to do.

VALUES. Your system of values will guide you as you follow God's way. But personal values are not created in a vacuum; they are formed in the context of community. The writer of Hebrews says, "Let us not give up meeting together . . . but let us encourage one another" (10:25 NIV). We learn new values from others, and others support us in living out our values. Stay close to people who share your values.

ACCOUNTABILITY. Cars and airplanes have gauges, which constantly report the status of the engine and warn of malfunctions. Companies are periodically audited to inform their directors of needed corrections. In the same way, you need to be held accountable by others who will monitor your progress and keep you on track. You need people on your team who are interested enough to ask the tough questions: How is your faith doing? Where are you failing? What kind of help do you need?

How Strong Is Your Cord?

Solomon described a support team this way:

Two are better than one, because they have a good return for their work: If one falls down, his friend can help him up. But pity the man who falls and has no one to help him up! Also, if two lie down together, they will keep warm. But how can one keep warm alone? Though one may be overpowered, two can defend themselves. A cord of three strands is not quickly broken (Ecclesiastes 4:9–12 NIV).

Who comprises your "cord of three strands"? Who are people in your life who are there for you, pulling for you, not afraid to tell you the truth? Which friends are available to comfort you when you are down, show you more about God than you already know, and bring you up short when you are headed for trouble? Who can you count on to guide you when you don't know what to do, cry with you when you lose, and then celebrate with you when you win?

There are two kinds of people around you: those who are growing personally and those who are going nowhere and stagnating. Welcome as traveling companions people who are pursuing God and his way for them, because they are constantly growing. They will help keep you on the way God has made for you. Do not entrust your heart to those who are stagnant or going backward. They can kill your dreams and turn you away from God's way.

> Welcome as traveling companions people who are pursuing God and his way for them, because they are constantly growing.

You may already have in your life a person or two who meets your need for support. If so, thank them for their ministry to you. Also explain that you need them in order to make the next steps on your journey. Ask if they will be available to provide accountability, feedback, or support. They will probably feel honored and valued that you would ask.

If you are running short of supportive friends, begin looking for a few. You may want to start by joining a structured support system, such as a Bible study group. Share with these people your dreams and struggles, and ask for their prayers and input. You will be amazed how a loving support group will help you on your journey.

Hopelessness is replaced
by hope, and we get
back on track again.

PRINCIPLE 3

Place High Value on Wisdom

When we are hopeless, a key way out of that hopelessness is to find the missing pieces of wisdom that would help put life back together. Many times we are in despair because we lack vital information about our condition and its cure. When we begin to discover and apply these key insights to our lives, our outlook changes. Hopelessness is replaced by hope, and we get back on track again.

So our third principle for finding God's way through your difficulties and challenges is this: *Recognize the value*

{ 19 }

and need for the missing pieces of wisdom in your life; then ask God to show them to you and help you search actively for them.

> God has put you in a universe of order.

There is information out there that will make all the difference in how you view your situation and how you can change it. Set out to find this information, and keep looking for it until you do. This step may not seem very spiritual to you, but it is something God has given you to do. In the meantime, he will do what only he can do to put your puzzle together.

A Word to the Wise

God says in Proverbs that wisdom produces hope: "Know also that wisdom is sweet to your soul; if you find it, there is a future hope for you, and your hope will not be cut off" (Proverbs 24:14 NIV).

When you feel hopeless, often it comes from a sense of not knowing what to do in your situation or feeling that nothing can be done. In reality, God *will* make a way. You just don't see it at the moment. As you learn more about what you are going through and apply what you learn to your situation, you will be exercising wisdom.

Wisdom Comes from God

The first place to look in your quest for wisdom is God himself. When you are in trouble or don't know what to do in a situation, the Bible instructs us to ask God for the wisdom we need. James writes this:

> *Consider it pure joy, my brothers, whenever you face trials of many kinds, because you know that the testing of your faith develops perseverance. Perseverance must finish its work so that you may be mature and complete, not lacking anything. If any of you lacks wisdom, he should ask God, who gives generously to all without finding fault, and it will be given to him (James 1:2–5 NIV).*

God knows what to do even when you don't. All you have to do is ask him for answers and he will provide them. Asking God is the first step to gaining wisdom.

God Uses Others

You may be in a situation you don't know how to handle. The good news is that there is somebody out there who does know how to deal with it, someone with the right knowledge and experience. After asking God for wisdom, your next task is to find that someone. With God's help and perhaps some diligent searching on your part, you will find the resource you need. Whenever I (Henry) am dealing with a difficult financial situation, I call a certain friend of mine. He has great wisdom in that area, and I lean heavily on him for good advice. There are other people I call for other needs.

You are wise to seek out people who have knowledge, expertise, and experience where you don't. Are you dealing with a rebellious teenager? Find someone in your church who may have good advice or who can refer you to a good counselor. Are you depressed over the loss of a loved one? Look for someone who has been through the stages of grief and can help you through your grieving. Whatever your challenge, others have been there and through it. Keep asking around until you find them.

Seek Structured Wisdom

Sometimes the situations we face require more than phone calls to friends or good advice from others who have been there. We need more professional sources of wisdom. For example, a person dealing with a clinical depression needs psychological treatment. Someone caught in an addiction needs a trained counselor in that area. You are wise to explore all the avenues of structured, professional help in your area of difficulty.

And there are a great number of services and pro-grams out there, if you know where to look. There are grief programs, substance abuse programs, divorce recovery programs, couples groups, debt relief counselors, resume writing and job interview coaches, and much more. You don't need to reinvent the wheel in your situation. There is probably an organization already in place ready to help you. You just have to find it.

Some people use cost as an excuse not to take advantage of structured, professional help. Yes, there may be a financial burden to bear when seeking help. But there are also a number of free programs around, and financial assistance from the government and other agencies is often available. Part of the journey is ferreting out all your possibilities.

So we urge you to actively and tenaciously seek the wisdom you need from the myriad of resources available. Here is just a sampling of places to start looking:

- Professionals in your area of need
- Self-help groups
- Pastors

- Churches equipped with programs for many different needs
- Community colleges
- Seminars
- Books, tapes, and videos
- Workshops
- Retreats

One caution: Make sure the sources you uncover are authentic. Don't believe every "expert." Look at their track record. Get referrals from people you know and trust—your friends, your support group, your doctor, your pastor, or other authorities.

The Order of Things

God has put you in a universe of order. The principles he established govern relationships, your work, the way you feel, and every aspect of your life. Things work or don't work because of the laws God set in place at creation. Proverbs says, "By wisdom the LORD laid the earth's foundations, by understanding he set the heavens in place; by his knowledge the deeps were divided, and the clouds let drop the dew" (Proverbs 3:19–20 NIV).

God will make a way for you. But part of that way has already been made in how he created life to work. Your task is to find his way by finding the wisdom that applies to your situation. You can depend on his ways to work and to make a way for you. So ask him for his wisdom and his way, then search for them with all your strength and apply them wholeheartedly.

You can depend
on his ways to work and to
make a way for you.

Examine your ways of
dealing with people
and problems which may
be trapping you in the past.

Leave Your Baggage Behind

Don't you hate dragging a load of luggage through an airport? How would you feel if you had to tote a couple of suitcases, carry-on bags, and backpacks wherever you went? What torture! You sure wouldn't get very far, very fast.

Similarly, on the journey along God's way, you won't get very far, very fast if you are loaded down with a lot of emotional baggage. *Our fourth principle for finding God's way to success in your life is to leave your baggage behind.* The more junk you jettison from your past, the easier it will be to navigate through the future.

What kind of baggage are we talking about? Let me (Henry) answer by introducing a concept we call *finishing*.

From the time we are born we all experience difficult, painful events and relationships. For example, someone hurts you physically or emotionally, your parents divorce or a mate divorces you, you make a serious mistake that hurts someone, you lose a loved one in a tragic accident. Ideally, these painful events are resolved in good time. Offenses are confessed, offenders are forgiven, conflicts are resolved, and the incident is finished. We no longer have to carry those burdensome fears and feelings.

However, many times our hurts do not get resolved as they should. Pain is stuffed instead of dealt with. Offenders are not forgiven, fears are not confronted, conflicts are not resolved. In other words, there is no appropriate finishing. As a result, we carry with us from the past feelings and patterns of behavior which impact our relationships and activities in the present, often in a negative way. That's baggage, and baggage doesn't go away until it is dealt with, or *finished*.

Tips for Finishing the Past

God has wired us to process pain and disappointment as it happens in our lives. Most of us didn't know that as children; so we have dragged suitcases full of unresolved issues into adulthood. Indeed, some of your baggage is directly related to the problems for which you are seeking God's way of helping or healing.

God will make a way for you, and part of that way involves helping you get rid of the baggage in your life. Here are a number of practical tips for helping you finish once and for all what has been left unfinished.

1. Agree That You Have a Painful Past.

I (Henry) have seen people overcome all kinds of pain from their past with God's help, so I know you can. But you won't overcome anything until you admit it exists.

Until you can acknowledge that painful things have happened to you—things which were not appropriately finished—you cannot work through them. And if you don't work through them, they will continue to disturb you in the present. So the first step to dealing with baggage is to confess to yourself and to God that you have issues that must be dealt with.

2. Include Others in Your Healing and Grieving.

The next step is to seek from others the care and healing you need to finish whatever happened in the past. It begins with opening up your feelings to others about what happened in the past so they can comfort you, pray for you, and encourage you. Pouring out your hurt to others who love you opens the door to the healing and support you need.

God's process of healing our pain, hurt, and loss usually involves grieving. Solomon wrote, "Sorrow is better

than laughter, because a sad face is good for the heart"
(Ecclesiastes 7:3 NIV). Don't feel ashamed if tears flow during the healing process. The Bible tells us to "weep with
those who weep" (Romans 12:15). Your tears, and the com-
passionate tears of those who love you, will help you let
go of your baggage.

3. Receive Forgiveness.

Often the pain we drag into new situations is from a
failure in the past. In order to get rid of your baggage, you
need to be free of the guilt and shame of past mistakes,
failures, and sins. Once you know
you are totally accepted, forgiven,
and loved, you can tackle life with
gusto.

> Forgiveness is about resolving the past.

True love and forgiveness come
from God. He promises to com-
pletely forgive you for anything and everything you
have ever done, no matter how bad you may feel it was.
The Bible promises, "For as high as the heavens are

above the earth, so great is his love for those who fear him; as far as the east is from the west, so far has he removed our transgressions from us" (Psalm 103:11–12 NIV).

So if you feel badly about something you have done in the past, ask God to take it away from you. His forgiveness and grace are always available, ready to give you another chance whenever you ask for it.

Your past failures and mistakes may have alienated you from some people as well as from God. Your hurtful words or damaging actions may have made you a few enemies. If so, God's way for you is to go to those people and make it right. Humbly confessing your wrong and receiving forgiveness from those you have hurt is a vital step to leaving your baggage behind.

4. Forgive Others.

Some of the baggage you carry is the result of being hurt by others. You may be the victim of a parent's lack of love and acceptance. Or perhaps you were betrayed by a spouse, abandoned by a friend, dishonored by a child, or misled by a spiritual leader. You were wronged in some way, and you still carry the pain, anger, and perhaps hatred from that offense.

If you are going to leave your baggage behind, you must forgive those who have wounded you. Take your cue from God, who has forgiven your sins. If you don't forgive, your resentment will continue to eat away at your heart and keep you from the freedom you seek on God's way.

Your forgiveness of others does not mean you deny that someone has hurt you, nor does it mean you must trust that person again. The future of your relationship depends on many factors. But forgiveness is about resolving the past. It is about clearing up what has already happened. It is about canceling the debt someone owes you. That's what it means to forgive. You are saying that the offender no longer owes you, that you are releasing him or her from all grudges, penalties, and retribution.

So leave the baggage of past hurts behind. Forgiveness is your ticket of freedom to go forward in your life.

5. Examine Your Ways.

Another part of your baggage relates to patterns of behavior we learned in past, painful situations.

You may have learned dysfunctional patterns for dealing with life, relationships, risk, and love, and these patterns are causing you problems now and holding you back from what God has for you. Take a close look at how you live. If you have trouble allowing people to get close to you, examine that pattern to see how it is limiting your relationships. If you tend to avoid conflict, examine that pattern to see how it is actually prolonging conflict. If you have learned to avoid any risk in an attempt to control your environment, notice how that pattern has imprisoned you.

Behavior patterns from your past may be ruining your present life. Examine your ways of dealing with people and problems which may be trapping you in the past.

Allow God to make a way for you into a better future by helping you let go of the patterns of the past.

6. See Yourself Through New Eyes.

Another kind of baggage we carry around is the distorted view of ourselves we learned in past relationships or situations. We see ourselves through the people who love us and sometimes through the eyes of those who don't. Our self-concept is a relational vision. We tend to look at ourselves through the eyes of others who are important to us. This is why some people suddenly blossom in healthy new relationships where they are valued as God's creation. It is also how other people grow to loathe themselves in relationships where they are devalued and mistreated.

How do you see yourself? Is your self-view realistic? Is it balanced with strengths and value as well as weaknesses and growth areas? Do you see yourself as loved?

If you are going to move forward in your life and find God's way for you, you must begin to see yourself realistically through the eyes of those who really love you. Begin by taking a look at yourself through God's eyes, for he loves you unconditionally and values you highly. Add to this the images you get from your dearest and most trusted relationships—those who love you as God does. This *new you* will begin to replace the distorted picture that has caused you such grief.

Leave the Past in the Past

In the Bible, when God rescued Lot and his wife from wicked Sodom and Gomorrah, he warned them against looking back. But Lot's wife was unable to let go of people and things in her past. She looked back and turned into a pillar of salt (see Genesis 19:17–26). Jesus used her as an example when teaching us to let go of harmful things that keep us from him. He said, "Remember Lot's wife!" (Luke 17:32 NIV).

Holding on to the baggage of the past will disable you for your journey with God. His way out is to deliver you from the hurt, forgiveness, and dysfunctional patterns of your past. Ask him to show you how to leave your baggage behind.

God is there with you,
empowering you to do
what achieves his ends.

Own Your Faults and Weaknesses

All of us play the blame game. We inherited this fault from Adam, who pointed the finger of blame at Eve, who in turn blamed the devil (see Genesis 3:11–13). Perhaps your eagerness to shirk blame has caused some problems in your life and relationships too. *Our fifth principle for finding God's way is that you take responsibility for your life, own up to your faults, and accept blame where it is justified.*

This principle means that for your life, the buck stops here, with you. Whatever you need in life, whatever you desire to happen, or whatever problem you try to solve, you are responsible for it. You need to step up to the plate and take charge. It's your job to call on God to make a way where you need a way. It's your job to do what he gives you to do. And it's your job to accept the blame when you fail.

The apostle Paul wrote, "Continue to work out your salvation with fear and trembling, for it is God who works in you to will and to act according to his good purpose" (Philippians 2:12b–13 NIV). Now that God has saved you, it is your responsibility to live a life which reflects him and his principles. But notice that you are not alone in your efforts. God is there with you, empowering you to do what achieves his ends. And it is this partnership—you doing your part and God doing his part—that will help you discover God's way for you.

When It's Not Your Fault

Some of the problems we face are not our own doing; we are the innocent bystanders caught in the crossfire. A competent, hardworking man is laid off because the economy turns sour. A devoted wife endures a miserable life because of her deadbeat, controlling husband. Unfortunately, this is one of the tragic realities of living in a fallen world. Those who live responsibly still get wounded.

Sometimes we have to take responsibility for situations that are not our fault. The man who is unfairly laid off may grouse about it and claim that the world owes him a job. That won't get him anywhere. He has to own up to the situation and start looking for another job. The unhappy wife may think she is justified in pining her life away. It won't make

> The way he makes for us is his way, not ours.

her any happier. She has to take responsibility for her situation and seek marriage counseling, whether her husband joins her or not.

Determining who is at fault in your situation isn't nearly as important as determining who will do something about it. The latter "who" is you. Whether you are fully to blame, partially to blame, or free of blame for the problems you face doesn't matter. What matters is taking ownership through God's strength and wisdom to do something about it. As you do, God will make a way.

How to Take Charge

The reverse side of assigning blame is taking ownership. When we take ownership for what happens in our lives, we are empowered to make changes. Ownership frees us to do something, make plans, tackle hurtful situations, and right wrongs. People who take charge of their lives are active people with real initiative.

Ownership also provides freedom. You are no longer a slave to the past, to false hopes, to wishing someone else would change, or to dis-

> When we take ownership for what happens in our lives, we are empowered to make changes.

couragement and passivity. You are free to take risks and to test-drive some possible solutions.

Here are a number of areas where you can begin to take responsibility for your life. As you work with God in taking charge, you will find his way out of your difficult situation.

YOUR OWN HAPPINESS. Ask God to help you take ownership of whatever pain or discomfort you are experiencing. Then ask him to help you find relief.

SPECIFIC ISSUES. Determine the root cause of your problem. Is it a relationship disconnect, a faith journey, a job issue, or a habit that won't go away?

NEEDED RESOURCES. You must lead the way in digging up the resources you need to solve your problem. Gather all the help, support, comfort, and advice you can find. Call around to find people who have answers and encouragement.

WEAKNESSES AND OBSTACLES. Identify the areas where you don't have the strength you need to meet the challenge, then begin to develop those areas.

ACCOUNTABILITY. Submit yourself to a few people who will help keep you on task with your project of resolving a relationship issue, losing weight, finding a career, or whatever your need may be.

SUPPORT TEAM. Seek out friends who are full of compassion and comfort, but who will not let you shirk your responsibility for taking the next step in resolving your issues.

ONE DAY AT A TIME. Address the issues of today rather than obsessing about yesterday or hoping for rescue tomorrow. People who take charge of their lives know how to live in the present because it's all they have to work with.

The Blessings of Taking Charge

Rob and Sharon are a good example of what can happen when you take responsibility of your own life. When Sharon came to me (John) to tell me Rob had left her, she was in shock. She had no clue about what to do next or where to turn. Should she call Rob and try to reconcile? Should she get an attorney? What could she tell the children? I consoled her and prayed with her, but I offered no advice at that time.

In her despair, Sharon made the right call. She reached out to the God she loved and trusted, the one she needed more than ever before. Sharon prayed and simply asked God for help. Nothing happened right away. But Sharon kept praying and trusting and listening for God's direction. It was as if God were allowing her time to deeply own her plea and her heart's desires.

In a few days, something did begin to happen. Sharon felt something churning in her heart. As she explained it to me later, her feelings toward Rob began to change. Instead of feeling her usual disappointment and hurt about being abandoned by her husband, she felt something of the pain *she* had caused *him*. She recalled conversations with Rob which she had previously cited as examples of his failure. Now she remembered how she had unfairly blamed him while glossing over her part in the problem.

She recalled one night when Rob was struggling under the weight of job stress. In a rare moment of vulnerability, he had asked Sharon just to hold him for a few moments before they went to sleep. Sharon had been so angry at him that she said, "Maybe if you handled your job better you wouldn't need to be cuddled like a little boy." Then she turned her back to him and went to sleep.

God continued to open up Sharon's heart for several days. She was heartbroken at what she discovered. She could not believe how hurtful she had been. At the same time, she was gaining a deeper sense of appreciation and love for Rob. As she took ownership of her share of their problems, it seemed she could see more clearly his positive qualities—those elements of his character that drew her to him in the first place.

Then Sharon knew what she had to do. She sensed that she had to make things right between herself and Rob. So she called him and they met. She told him what had happened to her and how God was working in her heart. Then she sincerely apologized for many years of heaping blame on him while shirking the blame herself. It was the most difficult conversation she had ever had in her life.

Rob was stunned. He had come geared up for more of her anger and blaming. When he realized that Sharon was sincerely penitent, he began to open up his heart to her. They continued to talk and set things straight. Within a few days, Rob was back home.

But the happy ending doesn't end there. God led Sharon into another level of ownership. Having owned up to the *pain* she had caused Rob, she now began to take responsibility for the *patterns* in her life which had caused his pain. Sharon took charge of her disorganization, self-centeredness, unrealistic expectations of Rob, and defensiveness. As she did, God made a way for her by melting her heart and maturing her in these areas.

Rob as so impressed with Sharon's turnaround that he took charge of his own actions and responses. He began opening up to Sharon instead of retreating and shutting down. He talked to her about his problems and apologized when he let her down. Today they rejoice that God made a way for them through the despair of their blame and separation.

God could have sent an angel to Sharon and told her exactly what to do, but he didn't. Instead, over a period of time, God softened and healed Sharon's and Rob's hearts. It serves to remind us that we cannot predict what God's way will be. His plan and purpose for us cannot be reduced to a formula. The way he makes for us is his way, not ours. Our role is to seek him, to take charge of our own circumstances, and to trust him to do what only he can do.

Sharon made the right call. She reached
out to the God she loved and trusted, . . .
[She] prayed and simply asked God for help.

Welcome your problems
as gifts from God
to help you become
a better person.

Embrace Problems as Gifts

P roblems and crises are a part of life. Some people hit a problem and stop dead in their tracks. And that's where they stay—stumped, stymied, stuck. All they want is to get rid of the problem as soon as possible. There are other people who find something very useful in problems. They ask, "What can I learn from this experience? What does God want to change in me?" *This is our sixth principle for finding God in your life: Welcome your problems as gifts from God to help you become a better person.*

Whether the problem relates to career, relationships, health, emotions, or loss, we all tend to focus our energies on putting out the fire and making sure it doesn't flare up again soon. It may be a recurring chest pain you just hope will go away. It may be a disconnect in your marriage you are learning to cope with. It may be an eating problem for which you are trying various diets and plans. It's a problem, it's painful, and we want it gone. So that's what we concentrate on.

> God sees our difficulties very differently than we do.

Now, there's nothing wrong with trying to solve the problem and alleviate the pain. I (John) have a friend, Gary, who was suddenly out of a job, and he worked diligently to find another one. But the way out of his problem wasn't his first concern. Rather, he was primarily interested in seeing God's perspective of his problem and finding God's way through it.

The word "through" is important. God sees our difficulties very differently than we do. We might compare it to how differently a physician and a patient sometimes view pain. You come to the doctor in agony. You want a shot or a pill, something to make the pain go away, and you want it *now*. But your wise physician knows your pain is a sign of a deeper problem. He prescribes even more pain: surgery and physical therapy.

It's your choice: You can demand immediate relief, knowing that your physical problem will recur. Or you can go "through" the healing process and resolve the problem once and for all. That's the same kind of choice you face when dealing with life's problems and crises. God loves you completely and wants the best for you. But like your physician, *he is less concerned about your immediate comfort than your long-term health and growth.*

This is why we read in the Bible, "Consider it pure joy, my brothers, whenever you face trials of may kinds, because you know that the testing of your faith develops perseverance" (James 1:2–3 NIV). God's way is not *out* of your problems but *through* them. That's how we learn from our difficulties and find God's way.

So instead of looking for a way *out* of your problems, you may want to consider two other places to look which will get you *through* them: *upward* and *inward*.

Two Ways to Look at It

The first direction to look in order to find God's way through your problems is upward. You must turn the eyes of your heart toward God, his Word, and his ways. You won't need to look far, for he is waiting just beyond your own ability to resolve your difficulty. Like a lost child crying out to a parent, cry out to the One who knows the solution to your problem, the lessons to be learned, and the way to get you there.

Our tendency is to play it safe. We're a little uncomfortable relying on an unpredictable God. Yet God knows that our "safe" approach to problems dries up the soul. He invites us to look upward to all his opportunities and resources. He is like a storm raining down on a stagnant stream which has been clogged with debris. As the torrent floods the stream, the debris is broken up and the flow begins again.

The second direction to look in times of trouble is *inward*. Once you've looked up to God, he will take you on a journey into yourself to teach you valuable lessons. He will shine a lantern of truth into the recesses of your heart, illuminating attitudes, old wounds, fresh hurts, weaknesses, and perspectives where you need to submit to his touch.

Accepting Pain as Normal

Problems are also a gift in that they help us *normalize* pain, that is, expect pain as a regular part of life. When we are in the middle of a trial, whether it's a minor problem or a catastrophic loss, we protest or deny or argue that these things should not be. But none of it alters the reality of the pain we face. And the more we bluster, the harder it is to learn the first lesson of trouble: It must be accepted as a normal part of life.

You must give up your protest about pain and problems and come to a place of acceptance. Only then can you learn what choices, paths, lessons, and opportunities are available to you. You accept pain as part of life. You accept that problems will always be with you. You accept that you don't have all the answers. You accept that some problems will remain mysteries until we are face to face with God. Acceptance helps us live in God's reality, adapt and change to the way things really are, and trust him.

Indentification with Suffering

Our problems are gifts in another way. They help us identify with God's sufferings. God is not one to shrink from problems, nor does he avoid the difficulty they cause him. Though he could have created the world differently, he has chosen a path that brings suffering for himself. He deals with problems, even when they hurt him.

Ever since Adam and Eve, the human race has been a problem for God. He only wants to love and guide us, but we have walked away from him since time began. He doesn't want to destroy us and start over, because he loves us. Yet when he tries to draw close to us, we shake our fists in his face or attempt to be God ourselves. So God has this problem, since our response to his love is not what he desires.

God has a heart. He feels deeply, especially about us, and our rebellion hurts him. When Israel turned away from him, he responded, "My heart churns within Me" (Hosea 11:8). When Jesus saw Jerusalem's hard-heartedness, he yearned to gather its people to himself, but they refused his love (see Matthew 23:37).

God's response to his problem with us is to face it and take responsibility for doing something about it. He does not protect against, avoid, or deny the problem. Yet he suffers during the process. While we redeems, restores, forgives, repairs, and heals us, he suffers from what we put him through. When we learn how God addresses problems this way, we learn to identify or associate ourselves with his suffering. Throughout the ages, spiritual people have studied how identifying with his pain helps us draw closer to him, see life as it really is, and take a right approach to life's problems.

This is why there is much to be learned through problems as we allow ourselves to come closer to God's suffering, especially the sufferings of Jesus: "Let us fix our eyes on Jesus, the author and perfecter of our faith, who for the joy set before him endured the cross" (Hebrews 12:2a NIV). When we identify with God's sufferings, we are deepened and matured. Many people say that getting through a problem was not nearly as important as what they learned about suffering God's way.

Don't ask God to get rid of your problems, and don't merely tolerate them. Welcome them as gifts and you will find God's way through them. View your problems as the next steps of growth for you.

When we identify with
God's sufferings, we are
deepened and matured.

Time allows God's healing
ingredients to be applied
to our situation.

Take Life as It Comes

I (John) have a bone disease called osteopenia, meaning that my bones are too porous. Osteopenia, a precursor to the better-known osteoporosis, can lead to easy fracturing and slow healing. A couple of years ago, I broke my back in a hot air balloon accident in Kenya, and the doctors theorized that my back wouldn't have broken had I not had this condition.

Since my diagnosis, I have spent some time investigating treatments and cures. If it is avoidable, I would prefer not to grow old with brittle bones. My mother has osteoporosis, and it has not been easy for her to live with.

The good news is that much can be done to improve my condition. Experts recommend dietary supplements and daily bone-strengthening exercises. So my doctor has me on such a regimen. Every year I get an X-ray to determine if my condition is improving or deteriorating. Since bones change very slowly, it is futile to check progress more frequently. So I have to wait all year to see how I'm doing.

Living in the unknown for such a period has taken some adjustment. As I write this, my next X-ray is about six months away. So I keep up with the supplements and exercises, but I won't know if they're working for six months. I would love to get up-to-the-minute feedback, just like a dieter gets by stepping on a scale every day. But all I can do is hope that things will be better when the X-ray is finally taken. Until then, I wait.

The waiting is difficult, but I have learned something for it. My condition has taught me that I am not the master of time. I can't speed it up or slow it down. I am at the mercy of the clock and the calendar; so I must let time have its way.

A Matter of Timing

Our seventh principle for finding God's way in our lives relates to what I am learning through my osteopenia: *When God makes a way for us, it usually takes time, so we must allow time for God to work.* Though I believe deeply that God performs instantaneous miracles, it seems that with God's way, you must allow his process to happen.

Time plays a very important role in how God makes a way for us. *Time allows God's healing ingredients to be applied to our situation.* We need time to experience all the ways God may use to bring about change. We need thorough and repeated exposure to his love, truth, grace, and help. We don't generally learn things the first time around. And wounded hearts need additional time to implement the help God provides for them. Just as antibiotics effectively combat an infection over a period of days, so the healing of our lives may take a period of time. As such, time is a blessing, not a curse.

Fighting Against Time

Still, it's not easy to wait for God's solution. We tend to become impatient and childish when things don't happen when we want them to. We feel stretched, discouraged, frustrated, and sometimes ready to give up. We respond in a number of ways. Some people feel a desperate need for immediate relief in a painful crisis. Others believe that God will bring instant deliverance if they have enough faith. Some people feel out of control when they can't speed things up. Still others tend to be impulsive and cannot tolerate any frustration in getting what they need.

However, those who submit to time's restrictions generally find better results than those who protest against them or try to get around them. Those who insist on shortcuts and quick fixes tend to repeat the same problems over and over again, getting nowhere. But if a goal is meaningful, it will require time to reach it. Solomon wrote, "The plans of the diligent lead to profit as surely as haste leads to poverty" (Proverbs 21:5 NIV).

> We can know that he is working behind the scenes even when we can't see anything happening.

As difficult as it may be to wait on God's process, we can know that he is working behind the scenes even when we can't see anything happening. The following parable of Jesus illustrates the point:

> *This is what the kingdom of God is like. A man scatters seed on the ground. Night and day, whether he sleeps or gets up, the seed sprouts and grows, though he does not know how. All by itself the soil produces grain—first the stalk, then the head, then the full kernel in the head.*
>
> *As soon as the grain is ripe, he puts the sickle to it, because the harvest has come (Mark 4:26–29).*

According to the story, we have two tasks as God makes a way for us. First, we must sow whatever seed he gives us. In other words, do the things he tells us to do at the moment; take these small steps of faith. Second, wait patiently and hopefully for those seeds to sprout and produce fruit. Don't rush God's pace. Even when we have done all we can do, he is still at work to produce something good in our lives.

Time Alone Does Not Heal

An old saying may cause us to believe that "time heals all wounds." At best, it's only partially true. It is important to understand that time isn't the primary factor when God makes a way. Some people think all they need to do is be patient and wait for God to do something they desire. These people find themselves stuck in a holding pattern. They wait for God to change circumstances, for another person to come around, or for their feelings to be transformed, and they are disappointed when the change doesn't occur.

Time does not *cause* healing; it is simply the *context* for God's healing ingredients to interact with your situation. All the other elements that God uses to make a way are still necessary. You don't wait for a sprained knee to heal. You get a brace, do the stretches and physical therapy, and give it heat and massage. Time alone is rarely enough.

Time is the context for our *involvement in the process*. It helps me a great deal to become engaged in tasks, experiences, and relationships as I walk God's path for me. When you are part of whatever God is doing in your life, you are, in a sense, lifted out of time constraints to experience something of eternity where God lives. The more engaged you are, the less you will feel the pressure of time.

Surround yourself with all the love, truth, support, advice, safety, and accountability you need to do your part of the process. Time, along with the other healing components, will produce deep and long-lasting results.

The Seasons of Your Life

We often categorize time into seasons. As with the seasons of nature, there are different seasons of life. Solomon wrote, "There is a time for everything, and a season for every activity under heaven" (Ecclesiastes 3:1 NIV). We can better understand God's timing in his way for us when we understand the seasons of our lives and identify which season we are in now.

You need to cooperate with and adapt to the seasons of growth in your life in order to find God's way for you. The four seasons mentioned here relate to any situation or context of growth and struggle you may be experiencing.

WINTER. Cold weather and hard ground make this season appear dead and unfruitful. However, winter can be a very productive time. It's a time to clear the ground of the deadwood, debris, and stones that will hinder future growth. It's a time to mend fences and repair broken machinery. Winter is the time for making plans and preparations for the growing seasons.

You may want to use the seemingly dead season of your life to prepare for the work ahead. For example, spend time arranging your schedule, organizing your affairs, and setting goals. Research the resources you need, such as enlisting a support team, locating organizations and programs, and seeking out counselors. Winter helps you rest and get ready for growth.

SPRING. It's a time of new beginnings and fresh hope. You plow and aerate the soil, add fertilizer and supplements, plant seeds, and irrigate. As growth begins, you care for the fragile shoots that seem to appear like magic. You keep the garden free of birds and other pests which can ruin the crop.

In the spring of your life you get involved in the plans and commitments you made in the winter. You may start studying an area of needed growth or join a group that is working on the issue. And when you see positive changes peeking out of the soil, you may need to protect them from people and circumstances that could trample them or snatch them away.

SUMMER. Growth is apparent in summer as the fields are lush with healthy plants. You are in a maintenance mode, making sure that what began in the spring continues. The ingredients of growth and the elements of protection are still necessary.

In the summer of your personal growth, you must be diligent to keep going. Don't be lulled into inactivity because good things are happening. Stay with the program for the full harvest. Keep working at what God has given you to do.

FALL. At harvest time you reap what you have sown. You experience the benefits of your work and spend time gathering fruit to enjoy today and to store for the winter.

In the fall of personal growth, you will see positive changes in your emotions, behavior, relationships, career, or other areas you have been working on. These are not merely cosmetic; they are the product of an internal transformation. You are a new person in that particular area. It is a time of celebration and gratitude to God. It is also a time to give back something of what you have received in service to God and others.

I would rather skip the work of winter, spring, and summer and enjoy the harvest of fall all the time, wouldn't you? We want results now and are easily disheartened when we have to work or wait for them. It is not easy to submit to the tasks of the season we are in, waiting for the fall. But if you learn to adapt to the seasons instead of fighting against them, you will reap a bountiful harvest in due time.

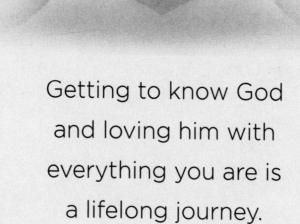

Getting to know God
and loving him with
everything you are is
a lifelong journey.

Love God with All You Are

God loves you unconditionally and desires to make a way for you through your difficult situation. Finding his way is also a matter of love on your part. *Our eighth principle for finding God's way is to love him passionately with every area of your life, including your pain, your fear, and your despair.*

Jesus said, "Love the Lord your God with all your heart and with all your soul and with all your mind. This is the first and greatest commandment" (Matthew 22:37–38 NIV). Loving God is the greatest commandment because it encompasses all his other rules for life. If we love God, connect to him, and follow him as he commands, we will value what he values and seek to do what honors him and is best for us.

When you're in a bad situation and don't know what to do, don't pull away from God. Draw closer! Love God in that situation. Invite him into your feelings, thoughts, actions, and reactions. Immerse yourself in his love, and you will find his way for you. Below are several important facets of your life where love for God must take the lead for you to find God's way.

VALUES. Our values determine what is important and unimportant to us. Loving God in this area means deriving our values from him. What is important to you? For example, God loves the person who has wronged you, even though he doesn't approve of that person's behavior. Adopting God's values means learning to love that person too, despite the pain he has caused you. When you don't love God with your values, you will have difficulty finding his way in your life.

PASSIONS. These deep urges and drives keep us feeling alive. When your passions are motivated by self and sin, they can get you into a lot of trouble. Passions out of control may result in addictions to alcohol, drugs, pornography, food, or something else. But when you turn your passions over to God, they can fire you up to do the right thing. Allow your love for God to fuel your passions.

EMOTIONS. God created you with a wide range of emotions, which can be expressed either positively or negatively. No matter how you feel in your situation—angry, depressed, anxious, desperate—ask God to flood your heart with his love so you will express these emotions in a healthy way.

HURTS. We all experience deep inner hurts at various times. People fail us, dreams are shipwrecked, circumstances go against us. God will make a way when you allow him into your wounds. You may avoid bringing him into your hurt, fearing that he will hurt you more or blame you for the hurt. But he understands your pain and will heal those wounds when you give them to him.

LOVE FOR OTHERS. Sometimes we love people who are good for us, and sometimes we love the wrong people or we love for the wrong reasons. When you bring your love for others to God, he will guide you to trust and invest your life in the right people.

MOTIVES. Our choices and actions in life are guided by our motives. Sometimes we are motivated to be caring, responsible, and free. At other time our motives prompt us to be self-protective, fearful, or selfish. Expose your motives to God so he can transform them into motives like his own.

SINS. We have all fallen short and missed the mark in life. We harbor sinful thoughts, speak sinful words, do sinful deeds. When you bring your sins to God, he freely forgives, heals, and provides a way to work through them and find victory and freedom.

TALENTS. God created you with certain skills, strengths, gifts, and talents so you can help others enjoy a better life. Love God with all your abilities. As you do, God will use you to make a way for others.

PREFERENCES AND OPINIONS. As a unique individual, you have your own set of likes and dislikes, preferences and opinions. You enjoy a certain kind of church or worship style. There are certain types of people you are drawn to as friends. Don't be afraid to bring your unique preferences to God. He will make a way for you to sort through your preferences and use them to make a better life.

God's Love Makes a Way

Think of the dearest, closest, most loving relationship in your life. It may be one you're in right now with a spouse, fiancé, parent, child, or dear friend. Or it may be a relationship from your past—a love lost, a friendship gone cold. What characterized this relationship at its best?

You were probably very open with each other at every level. You knew each other's best-kept secrets, darkest fears, and deepest desires. You took risks. You allowed yourselves to need and depend on each other. And this relationship made you feel alive. You were so close that you were almost indistinguishable from each other.

Our best, purest, and most rewarding human relationships are only a frail picture of the loving, intimate relationship you can enjoy with God. Getting to know God and loving him with everything you are is a lifelong journey. And the more of yourself you open up to him, the more God is able to make a way for you through your problems. *God will make a way for you to the extent that you make a way for him in your heart.*

That's what loving God is all about. It's saying to God, "Do whatever you need to do in my life." It's saying as Jesus did, "Not my will, but yours be done" (Luke 22:42b NIV). As you open yourself to him in this way, he has access to every part of you that needs his love, grace, and support.

Loving Your Way To Wholeness and Healing

When you love God with every part of yourself, he brings unity and wholeness to your life. Like a well-trained orchestra, every element of who you are—body, soul, spirit, mind, emotions, will, personality—works together for a beautiful outcome. You avoid the disharmony of loving God with your head while your heart is cold and distant, or loving God with your emotions while making wrong choices. Fully unleashing God's love in your heart brings unity and allows his love to flow through every part of you.

God's love also fulfills your need for healing. Life's problems, trials, and pains leave us injured emotionally, relationally, and spiritually. If you ever need God to make a way in your life, it's when you're suffering. But God is a healer by nature. He has the will and the resources to put your life back together again. As the psalmist writes, "He heals the brokenhearted and binds up their wounds" (Psalm 147:3 NIV).

> That's what loving God is all about. It's saying to God, "Do whatever you need to do in my life."

God is all about love, and he wants us to be all about

love too. He makes a way for those who love him with everything they have. The more you make yourself accessible to him, the more you can grow, be healed, and find his way. Whatever problem you are dealing with in life, make sure you are not hiding it from God. Love God with all your heart, soul, mind, and strength, and let his love set you free.

The more you make yourself
accessible to him, the more you can
grow, be healed, and find his way.

Getting to know God and
loving Him with
everything you are is a
lifelong journey.

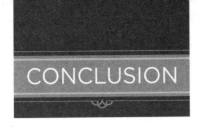

Begin Your Journey Today

You are near the end of this book, but you are only at the beginning of your journey of exploring and experiencing the way God is making for you. In the earlier chapters we have attempted to, as it were, fill your pack with supplies and put a map in your hands. Now it's time for you to hit the trail on your own two feet. As you do, we leave you with three final words of advice. Think of them as the three key elements on your hike: your two feet—right and left—and the trail ahead of you.

Walk in Grace

Your first step on the journey, and every subsequent step, is a step into God's grace. Simply put, grace is God's *unmerited favor*. "Favor" means that God is for you; he is on your side. He wants the best for you; he is on your side. He wants the best for you and is committed to work in you, with you, and

> God loves you completely, and he is excited about your journey.

through you to give you his best. God loves you completely, and he is excited about your journey. He's going with you every step of the way. He will be your biggest cheerleader.

Step Out in Faith

You need two strong legs to complete a strenuous hike—right, left, right, left, one after the other. Similarly, in

CONCLUSION: Begin Your Journey Today   { 87 }

your journey with God, faith is a two-step process. It is both an *attitude* and an *action*. You believe God loves you, but you need to love him in return. You know God will speak to you, but you need to listen attentively. You have faith that God will guide you and protect you, but you need to follow him and submit to his care. Whenever you take a step of *faith* in God, follow it with a step of *action*.

Hit the Trail

Now that your feet are moving, let's take a look at the trail ahead. This is the way God is making for you. It may be strenuous in trying times, but it is full of discovery and wonder. And the destination at trail's end is well worth the effort.

God is your gracious, fearless leader on this trek, but you have some responsibilities for the journey. Here are ten key reminders that will help keep you on the trail and moving forward.

1. SET GOALS. What do you want God to do for you? Decide now, and be specific. Make your goal as clear and concise as you possibly can. Envision it, pray about it, and decide on a specific strategy to reach it.

2. RECORD PROGRESS. Write down your goal and put it where you can see it often—on the fridge, on the bathroom mirror, in your daily planner or journal, beside your desk or work station. Also, write down each significant insight and step toward your goal.

3. GATHER RESOURCES. Start looking for the people, programs, and organizations who can assist you on the journey. The better your resources, the faster you should reach your goal.

4. ACQUIRE INFORMATION. Educate yourself on the issues you are facing. Studies show that medical patients who are more knowledgeable about their condition tend to do better in treatment. They ask insightful questions and sometimes notice things

doctors might miss. As much as possible, become an expert in the area of your struggle.

5. INDENTIFY TASKS. Give yourself specific assignments: thought patterns to adopt, actions to perform, emotions to express, and habits to form. Remember: This is a step-by-step journey. Break your tasks into manageable portions and take them one by one.

6. EVALUATE PROGRESS. Review your goal and progress at defined intervals. Are you making headway? If so, what are the contributing factors? If not, why not? Put your evaluation in writing for future reference, and make any necessary adjustments to your plan.

7. EXPLORE PREFERENCES. Feel free to tailor your plan and tasks to your individual preferences. You will likely have many choices on your journey: counselors, programs, classes, and organizations.

8. REMAIN FLEXIBLE. Don't cast your plan in stone. It exists to serve your growth. If your plan is not

bearing fruit in your life over a reasonable period of time, rethink it and make changes. And even when your plan is working, stay alert to ways you can improve it.

9. PRAY CONTINUALLY. When you pray, you're not talking to the wall or to yourself. You are talking to God, and he hears you and responds. Prayer is a genuine and powerful ally on your journey. It's not your prayers that have the power; rather, it's God on the other end of the line who has the power to do what you cannot do. Don't take one step without talking to God about it.

10. PACE YOURSELF. God's way for you is a journey, not a race. Few changes happen overnight, no matter how hard you may work or pray. Give God time to work, and be thankful for the little changes you see.

We are pleased that you are so interested in allowing God to make a way for you. We pray that the God in whom we live, move, and exist will guide and sustain you on the journey, both today and forever. God bless you.

HENRY CLOUD, PH.D.
JOHN TOWNSEND, PH.D.
Los Angeles, California

BONUS MATERIAL

Real Life Answers for Tough Situations

What to Do About Discouragement & Depression

Eric, a successful, married businessman in his late forties, came to see me (John) about a problem with depression. No matter what he did, he felt very down all the time—discouraged, hopeless, and with a lack of enjoyment in anything he did. It didn't make sense to him, for his life, while not perfect, was reasonably OK.

Eric was at the stage of life in which things should

have been getting smoother for him. His wife, Laura, and he were happily married. Their two children were in college, and the "high maintenance" years of parenting were behind them. His place in his company as a senior vice president of a home-building group was secure, and a good fit for him. So as far as life struggles went, there wasn't a lot to go on.

I asked Eric, "At this point, what have you done so far to deal with the depression?" He said, "Well, I have been praying a lot for God to help me and reading my Bible. And, since the kids are gone, I have more free time, so I volunteer at the church and I've started playing golf. Thought that would give me a lift. But nothing really helps. I still feel like I'm swimming in mud most of the time. It's just awful."

I empathized with Eric. If you've never experienced true depression, you wouldn't wish it on your worst enemy. It is a darkness inside of you that you cannot get away from or talk yourself out of.

"What about your relationships?" I asked.

"You mean friends? I have a good group of guys that I play golf with."

"How do they handle your depression?"

"Well," Eric replied, "that's not the sort of thing we really talk about. I think that's a pretty personal subject. Besides, they would think I'm nuts, being depressed with the kind of life I've got."

I asked, "So who knows how you feel?"

Eric thought a minute. "Well, Laura does, but she feels pretty helpless about it. She doesn't know what to do, so she tries to help me see the positive things in life and stay active. And God knows my insides, of course. He's the one I want to heal me."

"What if I told you," I asked, "that you need more than just God in that place?"

"I'd say that you were telling me that God isn't enough for me—and I have a problem with that."

"Well, I agree with you there," I said. "I do believe that God is enough to meet all our needs and solve all our struggles. However, the Bible teaches that God has designed us to not only open up to him and his love and grace but also to people who will be kind and safe with us."

Eric was a little confused. "I guess that still sounds like trusting man, not God."

So, to illustrate my point, I took Eric through several verses from the Bible, such as:

> . . . it is not good for the man to be alone. (Genesis 2:18 NIV)

> Two are better than one, because they have a good return for their work: If one falls down, his friend can help him up. But pity the man who falls and has no one to help him up! (Ecclesiastes 4:9–12 NIV)

> . . . we can comfort those in any trouble with the comfort we ourselves have received from God. (2 Corinthians 1:4 NIV)

I explained, "We all have a need for the grace of God, and also for the grace that he provides through other people. Without it, we don't have access to the under-standing, kindness, and support that he designed us to experience. And my hunch is that you are sort of out of gas, relationally speaking, since you didn't think it was OK to let others in. And that is a leading cause of depression."

Eric started putting the pieces together. "You know," he said, "the family I grew up in was a very loving one. My parents really cared. But at the same time, if I was afraid or lonely, it wasn't really OK to talk about that. They would just shrug those problems off and tell me to think better thoughts and stay busy."

"Sounds like life today," I said.

"It's a lot like today," Eric agreed. "I have always enjoyed my marriage and kids, and my friends and my work. But I never thought I should talk to anyone about my problems."

"Right," I agreed. "And it may be that now that the kids are gone and life has slowed a little, with less work stress, your circumstances have allowed your own relational isolation and emptiness to come out. That may be why this has happened at this juncture for you."

It made sense to Eric, and he got to work. He started concentrating on his fears of letting others in. He joined a small home group at church that was into relationships. He began working on trusting others and letting them know him. It took some time, as he was used to talking to others about their lives but avoiding his own. But gradually, as he became connected on deeper levels to a few safe people, Eric began realizing his depression was resolving. He felt more energy, more hopefulness, and more life inside himself.

Eric's depression had served as a signal to him that he was very alone inside. Some depressions are signals for other issues, but this was his. And so, when he became grounded with people who cared and wanted to know his "insides," the signal was no longer needed, and the depression went away.

Depression, though painful, is quite a common condition. If you suffer from it, you are far from alone. And the good news is that when you don't know what to do about depression, there are effective and helpful answers and solutions—and a lot of sound hope—for your depression. Read on and find out.

Understanding Depression

When you face depression and don't know what to do or where to turn, God can make a way for you to overcome it—even severe and debilitating depression. God is no stranger to depression; he understands it, and his nature is such that the darker the despair, the more his love and light grow. He heals most where we are injured the most: "You, O Lord, keep my lamp burning; my God turns my darkness into light" (Psalm 18:28).

Out of Life

According to psychological and psychiatric researchers, depression can be identified by these symptoms:

- A depressed mood

- Changes in appetite
- Changes in sleep patterns
- Fatigue
- Self-image distortions
- Problems in concentration
- Hopeless feelings

When you experience even some of these symptoms over a period of time, you are depressed.

In addition to the emotional component, depression often has a medical component. During depression the brain chemistry is altered, and medication may be required to bring about the right balance of chemicals so that the person's brain can function correctly. When the brain needs corrective medication, it signals this need by the presence of what are called vegetative symptoms—that is, symptoms that affect a person's ability to function, live, and carry out life's responsibilities. Problems with sleep, appetite, and fatigue are examples of these sorts of symptoms.

When these are in play, no amount of talking or support will resolve the chemical issue. In computer terms, it is not just a software issue now; it is also a hardware issue. The brain itself is not working as it should. Depression that has a medical component must be treated with medication. So if you struggle with a severe depression, we encourage you to consult with a psychiatrist in order to look at the possibility of medications that can help alleviate your symptoms while you are addressing the emotional and relational aspects of your healing.

At its heart, depression is a spiritual, emotional, and personal condition. That condition is best described as being *cut off from life*. Some aspect of the person's heart and soul is out of order, disengaged and disconnected from God and others. It is as if some vital part of you is lost and frozen in time, and it is inaccessible for love, relationship, grace, or the truth.

God did not design or create us to be disconnected from himself or the life he wanted us to have. His intent from the beginning has always been that we should experience total love and joy. What, then, are the ways that God provides for you to deal successfully with depression?

Connecting the Disconnected

No matter what is causing or driving your depression, in order for the depression to lead you to life, you need relationship. Your soul needs to experience the depth and healing of love and grace. No one gets well on his or her own. Anyone struggling with depression will need to be connected, both to God and to people. The best place to be in any situation is in relationship. Relationship is not a luxury, it is a necessity. We are created as relational beings, and our well-being depends on relationships. And this is particularly true for you if you are depressed.

As we said earlier, a lack of connection and relationship helps give rise to the depression. The nature of depression requires that you be open and vulnerable to other safe people. The presence and application of relationship will help to undo your depression, because it will draw out the broken part of your soul and enable it to receive what it has been lacking.

As you likely recognize, this can be difficult. People who care about you and love you can surround you, and yet the isolated parts of your soul may remain untouched because you can't open up and receive the healing of their love for you. It will take time for you to recognize and reach the part of your soul that you have kept from others. Initially, you may not be able to "reach out and touch someone" with the broken part of yourself, because it may simply be too inaccessible, too hurt, or too undeveloped.

All you have to do—and we admit that this can be a lot—is reach out for relationship and connection with God and others and be committed to the process of healing, to God's path for you out of depression. You can bring yourself to relationship, even in a depressed state. The best you may be able to do is reach out to a group, a pastor, or a counselor who can give you some relational structure and tell them, "I have an aloneness inside. As I am now, I can't let you inside where it is. But I want to be as vulnerable and honest as I can so that, in time, the disconnected parts of me can also come into the relationship." Be open with those parts of your heart that you can be open with, and allow God, his love, and his people to help the rest happen.

Remember that relationship, as God has designed it, is most of what life really is. Allow relationship to fill, guide, and comfort you. That is a large part of what begins to heal and resolve depression.

As you seek connection with God and others, you should also begin exploring the cause of your depression.

Redeeming What Is Lost or Broken

As you ask God to help you identify the cause of your depression, remember that he always redeems his people who have lost their way or have lost some part of themselves. God is a redemptive God. That is why he is called "my Rock and my Redeemer" (Psalm 19:14), for that is who he is and what he does. He seeks out the lost, repairs them, and helps them re-enter life to the fullest.

Here is a brief list of some of the things that can cause depression. As you go over it, see if any of these causes resonate with you. Ask those who know you if any of them make sense for your condition. And ask God to open windows inside you to help you find what is true about you:

Inability to grieve losses. This is a very common cause of depression. When you do not have the capacity to experience your sadness over your losses in life and let go of those things you have lost, the "frozen losses" keep you stuck. That is why, when people become safe enough to feel sad about who or what they no longer have in their lives, they go through a period of grief and then the depression resolves. That is why depression and grief are so different and should not be confused with each other. Actually, grief, which may seem like depression when you are in it, is the cure for many kinds of depression.

Lack of ability to need and depend on others emotionally. Some people have been disconnected from love and comfort all their lives. Their inner world is an empty, isolated place where they cannot reach out to anyone for their needs.

Problems in responsibility and freedom. There are times when a person has trouble taking ownership and control of his or her life, or does not feel free to choose what is right for him or her.

Burnout. For some reason, some people give to others beyond their resources, and even have difficulty receiving what they need in order to continue.

Perfectionism. The perfectionist will often become depressed as the reality of his or her failings and weaknesses becomes too much to bear.

Feelings of self-condemnation. This is an individual's suffering an unbiblical, over-critical, and harsh conscience that attacks him or her even when he or she has done no wrong.

Unresolved trauma. When a person has experienced a catastrophic event or injury that is not processed, confessed, grieved, and worked through, it can contribute to depression.

Medical causes. Some depressions are caused or influenced by a problem in brain chemistry, as we mentioned previously, or by other medical conditions that produce depression. Make sure you have adequate medical input here. A complete physical by a general practitioner and a psychiatric workup by a psychiatrist might be in order.

As you seek to discover which part of you has been lost, think of it as a part of you that you need in order to function well in life. Then, as that part emerges in the context of warm, safe, and loving relationships, begin allowing yourself to feel the feelings that go along with it. Experience the hurt that made that part disappear in the first place. Keep exposing it to the nurture and care of relationships. As it strengthens, take small risks with it. Learn to use it again in your life. Let it take its place in your world. Over time, allow that part of you to mature, grow up, and simply be a part of you that you again own, utilize, and experience.

Clearly, doing this will require a mentor. You will need someone who has good experience with depression, as there is a great deal to know about it. Find such a person and follow his or her guidance, and God's, as the part of you that is lost becomes found.

Depression can be debilitating and frightening. However, God is right there with you in the black hole, as he fills it up with love and light and provides a way out, back into his world. Trust him for that.

What to Do About Bad Habits & Addictions

Understanding Addiction

The hallmark of all addictions is that the person has lost control and is experiencing negative consequences as a result. Sadly, many of the activities that people become addicted to are things that God has designed to be a part of life, such as food, money, and sex. The problem comes when these things become consuming, so much so that the person loses his or her ability to control the use of them and becomes a slave of the behavior or substance. As the apostle Paul says, "'Everything is permissible for me'—but not everything is beneficial. 'Everything is permissible for me'—but I will not be mastered by anything" (1 Corinthians 6:12).

God understands that people can become addicted and that a person can actually become powerless over things in life. The loss of control is ultimately the kernel of addiction. Paradoxically, the loss of control is also the beginning of change—and of hope. When we admit that we are powerless to change, we can turn to God for help.

The Way Out

Jeri had been enslaved to binge eating for a long time. Her doctor had sent her to counseling because he feared greatly for her health. She was extremely overweight and had a history of heart disease in her family. So naturally he was quite concerned about her. She had tried many times before to control her eating through dieting. She would always lose some weight at first, but eventually she would give up and quit, only to have the weight that she had lost return, with a few extra pounds on top of it all. She didn't know what else to do. Despair had given way to detachment, and she found herself in a lonely pattern. She had given up. Yet the doctor had gotten her attention by explaining the seriousness of her situation, and she now feared for her very life.

When Jeri came to our clinic, the first thing we had to do was "cure" her of her commitment to dieting. She came in mistakenly believing that all she needed to overcome her eating problem was to have more resolve and willpower. This is not the way to work against addiction. Jeri had to learn that addiction was by definition *the inability to stop*. In other words, she had to learn to admit that she was powerless over her addiction and totally helpless to stop.

Next, Jeri had to learn that she had not truly reached out to God as the Source of power in her life of addiction. She had "prayed" about her problem many times, but that is very different than leaning on God as a source of power *in the addiction itself*. She had to learn that when temptation came, she had to pray and ask God at that moment for the strength to know what to do to flee the temptation.

Then, she had to learn that God also gives us strength through other people. She began to see that part of the reason she had failed before was that she had tried to go it alone. She had thought because she had joined diet groups emphasizing group support, that she was getting all the support she needed. She discovered that in moments of weakness, when she was feeling loneliness or self-pity, she needed to be able to call a few people. She needed a "buddy system." She learned to reach out to God and to a buddy and to talk things out rather than using food to make herself feel better.

As Jeri continued to work on things, she found that there were other dynamics driving her eating. She also had a fear of getting close to men because of some past abuse that she had suffered. She had subconsciously gained a lot of weight as a way of keeping men safely at a distance. She gradually became aware of these things that triggered her desire to eat, and she had to learn another way to express that pain instead of "eating it away."

In time Jeri came to understand that she had a few character flaws as well. She was not as honest as she thought she was. She was indirect with people and then held grudges and bitterness toward them instead of talking things out directly, offering forgiveness, and resolving conflict. She had always been a "nice" person, but that niceness was covering a lot of anger and resentment, and her true feelings would come out in her tendency to talk about people behind their backs. She had to learn to repent of that kind of indirect, hurtful behavior and to offer forgiveness and resolve conflict.

Jeri went back to school and started a new business, which became successful. She was soon hired as a consultant and was really thrilled that she was able to exercise her gifts and talents, overcoming a longstanding belief that she was "stupid" and unable to do anything significant. Now "significant" people were paying her to help them.

Oh, and one more thing: Jeri lost half her weight—and we do not mean half of her goal weight or half of the weight that she was supposed to lose. No, we mean *literally half of her body weight.* She went from 300 to 150 pounds. This was not as a result of a diet. She lost the weight as a result of getting connected to God and his life.

Here are the steps Jeri took to overcome her addiction:

- She got to the end of herself, the end of her own strength, and didn't know what to do about her addiction. She admitted her powerlessness.
- She found the strength she needed in reaching out to God.
- She found strength from God in reaching out to God's people.
- She overcame her aloneness and isolation through learning how to be vulnerable and to connect with others—this healed the pain that her eating was serving to medicate.

- She grew in her character, learning how to be honest, to be responsible, and to set good boundaries with others instead of being so passive and powerless.
- She grieved a lot of hurt.
- She forgave a lot of people and gave up a lot of bitterness.
- She developed her talents, reached out, took some risks, and grew a life of work and service.
- She learned to pray at a deeper, more realistic, and more dependent level.
- She began to study the Bible in a different way, not as a religious obligation but as the place to find the wisdom that was healing her.
- She learned new interpersonal skills for building better relationships.
- She worked out conflicts with people, asked for forgiveness, and made amends.
- She learned to reach out to people at the critical times when she needed help.
- She lost the weight—150 pounds of it!

These steps map the path that God prescribes and that Jeri took. She got to the end of herself, reached out to God, and with his help got reconnected to him and his life. He healed her, removed things from her soul and character that were hurting her, and built into her life some dynamic new things that she did not possess before going into her recovery. Through spiritual growth, her addiction was overcome.

From Hope to Certainty for You Too

If some part of your life is out of control and resulting in negative consequences, you may be struggling with an addiction. If so, you are a candidate for recovery. Here is a summary of the steps you can take to find help and healing. You will notice that many of them are the same as the twelve steps of Alcoholics Anonymous.

1. Admit to yourself, to God, and to another trusted person that you are out of control and this addiction has gotten the best of you. Admit that you are powerless on your own to fix it.

2. Ask God for forgiveness for whatever you have done, and claim it. Receive it as true and real, and get rid of all self-condemnation.

3. Believe that God can help you, reach out to him, and totally submit yourself to his care, guidance, direction, and strength. Submit and commit yourself to total obedience to whatever he shows you to do.

4. Take an ongoing inventory of all that is wrong inside yourself, as well as between you and others. Broaden the scope of the self-investigation to include all that you have done wrong. Confess it to God and to someone else that you trust.

5. Continually ask God to show you any problem or deficiency in your life that you need to work on. And when he does tell you, follow through and work on it.

6. Go to everyone you have hurt and ask for forgiveness and make amends to them. Be judicious in doing this and make exceptions where bringing up buried things from the past might harm the person.

7. Seek God deeply. Ask him what he wants you to do; ask him for the power to do it, and then follow through in total obedience.

8. Reach out to others for help in overcoming your addictive behavior—especially to others who have gone through the problem and experienced victory.

9. Be alert and identify all the triggers that get your addictive behavior started. Then when they occur, that's the time to reach out. Do not ever underestimate the need to reach out. Recognition of this need is why some addicts, especially in the beginning, go to multiple meetings every day and have a sponsor who they can call at any time.

10. Dig deeply and discover inside yourself the hurts and pains that you are trying to medicate with your addiction and seek to have them healed. Find out what you are lacking inside and begin to reach out and receive the love and strengthening that you need.

11. Do not try to do all of this alone. Join a support

system, and maybe attend every day for a few months. Line up a few buddies you can call on every day for a while, and any time you need them later.

12. Find out what relational skills you need to develop, improve, or repair in order to make your relationships work. Work on these skills and take risks in order to relate to people better.

13. Forgive everyone who has ever hurt you.

14. Assess yourself to discover what talents you have and develop them. Put them to work pursuing your deepest dreams and goals.

15. Simplify your life so that it has less stress, and make sure that you are getting adequate rest and recreation and taking care of yourself mentally, emotionally, and spiritually.

16. Join a structured group that will provide the discipline you need to accomplish all of this.

17. Study God's Word and other spiritual writings that will teach you how to apply it.

18. Stay humble, be honest, and remember that spiri-

tual growth and recovery are for a lifetime, not just for a season.

19. If you are addicted to a substance, seek medical help as well. In the beginning of your treatment for substance abuse, it is possible that you will go through withdrawal or other serious medical conditions. Make sure that you have the professional supervision and counsel to do this safely.

20. See your addiction not as the central problem but as a symptom of a life that is not planted and growing in God. Get into recovery as a total life overhaul, not just to fix a symptom.

It does not matter what you are addicted to—a substance, a person, a behavior, or something else. It does not matter how long you have been addicted. It does not matter how severe the consequences. When you don't know what to do about it, God will provide a way. All you have to do is stop trying to tell yourself to be strong, admit that you are weak, and get into his system of recovery. The plan works if you work with the plan. The strength will not come from you but from God. Yet you have to go to him with your weakness and join his program in order to receive his strength. We encourage you to do that and to discover, like millions before you, that no matter what your situation, God can help you make a way out of your addiction.

What to Do About
Sex and Intimacy

Sexual difficulties in marriage can be a devastating experience. Couples who find that their romantic intimacy isn't working—for whatever reason—go through tremendous emotional and relational pain. They wonder if they are really in love, or if they are damaged beyond repair. They start to give up hope that they will ever feel the completion and deep connection that comes with a loving and sexual marriage.

One couple I worked with, Dan and Linda, were almost

at the end of their marriage because of a sexual conflict. Though she loved Dan, Linda simply had very little sexual desire for her husband. She never approached him for sexual relations, and whenever he took the initiative, she would either try to avoid it or simply endure the experience. On his part, Dan was extremely hurt and frustrated by this and often felt like giving up on the relationship.

As I got to know the couple, I became aware of a pattern in their relationship that seemed significant. Though he loved Linda, Dan was pretty controlling with her. He told her what to do and "called the shots" quite often. And Linda seemed to simply take it. She took a more compliant and docile role, as it helped them to avoid butting heads and having conflict.

I knew this sort of dance between two people often makes one spouse feel like a child and the other a parent. The "child" feels helpless and choiceless, and the "parent" feels in control and sometimes alone without an adult partner. Neither spouse feels really happy with the child-parent pattern.

I also knew that many problems in sexual unrespon-siveness are associated with this pattern. Kids aren't designed to want to have sex with their parents, so often the powerless spouse can't feel arousal or desire. She can't access her adult libido with her mate.

I told Dan and Linda what I was thinking. Linda thought it made sense. Dan was a little resistant, until I said, "So you can decide to keep things as they are, feel in control, and not regain sex and passion. Or you can give up some of the power, give half to Linda, and stand a good chance of regaining sexuality." When he saw it in that light, his incentive went up!

Dan began to encourage his wife's input, thoughts, and feelings. He stopped resisting her freedom as a person. Linda herself began to speak up more. She started dis-agreeing with Dan and confronting him when she needed to. It was a little rocky at first, for they weren't used to this. But pretty soon, Linda began feeling desire for Dan as she regained the adult role and position. Dan was grate-ful for the changes and felt that he'd had to give up very little to have a great marriage restored. I agreed with his analysis. It is also a symbol of a deep spiritual reality: what we give up to God, we are repaid for many times over.

If you are having sexual conflicts in your relationship, take heart. God makes a way for us all, in every path of life, and that includes the sexual arena. He created and designed the sexual experience, and he is very much "for" it. He has provided answers for your struggle in this book, and they work—if you engage in the process. Listen to him, learn from him . . . and watch what happens to the sex you have wanted to experience.

Love: The Foundation

A healthy sex life begins with love. Love brings a couple together and allows sex to flourish. Love encompasses sex; it's larger than sex. Love can create the desire for sex, but when the momentary passion of sex is over, love remains. It continues and is present with the couple, holding them close to each other and to the Author of love himself.

Love involves the whole person: heart, soul, mind, and strength (Mark 12:30). Love and sex both require an emotional connection between two people, which means both should be emotionally present and available. When two people can attach to each other in their hearts, a healthy sex life will emerge and develop. Yet when a couple lacks this kind of intimacy, their sex life will become atrophied because it cannot feed off the emotional connection. This can happen in several ways. Sometimes one mate will withdraw love out of anger, hurt, or a desire to punish the other. At other times one will be unable to take in or receive the other's love. Still other times one mate may have an inability to live emotionally in the world. Both people's hearts must be available in order to connect emotionally. If this is not the case, while sex can occur, it more often than not does not have enough fuel to be enflamed.

It's also true that love, and healthy sexuality, cannot exist without trust. Because sex is such a symbol of personal exposure and vulnerability, a healthy sex life requires that couples develop a great deal of trust in each other—trust that one partner will not use what he or she knows to hurt the other. When people trust each other, they feel free to continue their explorations of one another at deeper and deeper levels. In fact, one of the Hebrew words for trust also means "careless." In other words, when you trust someone, you can, in one sense, be *careless* with him or her. Of course, by careless we don't mean you can neglect the other's needs and feelings, but rather that you need not be anxious and fearful, editing what you say and feel. You are free to be yourself with the other person, because you can trust that he or she will not do wrong by you.

On the other hand, broken trust will often create sexual problems. This breach of trust doesn't even have to involve anything in the sexual arena, such as an affair or emotional unfaithfulness, though these can certainly be devastating to a relationship. A breach of trust can have to do with a financial matter, such as not being dependable with money, or it may be a commitment matter, such as promising something and not following through with it.

Broken trust can greatly diminish a person's desire for sex with a spouse. The deficit in emotional safety translates into a deficit in sexual safety. All of the techniques in the world will not cure a sexual problem caused by a breach of trust. Only God's solution of repentance, ownership, and rebuilding trustworthiness can accomplish it.

Ownership: Sharing the Sexual Partnership

In healthy marriages, both people wholeheartedly take ownership of whatever they are supposed to do. Both take responsibility for themselves as individuals and as part of the marriage. When both people take ownership in the marriage, it creates a context for healthy sex. Ownership involves shared responsibility, separateness, and self-control. Let's examine what each of these mean.

1. *Ownership means shared responsibility.* Responsibility is an aphrodisiac to a healthy person. For example, when a wife experiences that her husband is who he says he is, is dependable, and shoulders the burdens of his life, she experiences freedom. It frees her from the job of being alone with all

the weight of the world and the marriage on her, because she has someone with whom to share the load.

She is also free to be more sexual, as part of good sex is the ability to abandon oneself. Because she's free, she feels lighter and younger and has more emotional energy for sexual connection. When concerns about his responsibility are taken away, sex has room to exist in her mind and imagination.

2. *Ownership means separateness.* Ownership, by definition, creates space between two people—separateness. When two people take responsibility for their lives, they are defining themselves as individuals. They are saying, in effect, "I love you, but I am not you. You have your feelings, values, and opinions, and I have mine. Let's put them together and make something better as they interact."

Separateness helps each person in a marriage to assist the other's growth. One has a strength from which the other can learn. One has feedback and perspective that the other one needs to hear. This can certainly cause some conflict, but not all conflict is bad (Proverbs 27:17). As the saying goes, "If you never disagree, one of you is unneces-sary." More than this, however, *separateness creates the longing that is required for sexuality.* Sex is about two people being drawn to each other. Therefore, it follows that for good sex to develop, there needs to be two clear, distinct, well-defined "others"—two distinct people in the equation. There is space between those two people. Desire and longing have room to grow, and each wants the other person.

3. *Ownership means self-control.* Self-control, a fruit of the Spirit's work in our lives (Galatians 5:23), has to do with things like having our values dictate our behavior and attitudes, as opposed to allowing our impulses, instincts, and appetites to control them. People without self-control tend to be out of control or are controlled by something else. People who are self-controlled make their decisions based on their heart, soul, and mind all coming to a con-clusion about something.

Self-control has a great deal to do with sexuality, as sexual impulses are, at their core, oriented to *now.* Like a small child, our raw, unregulated sexual impulses demand instant gratification and release. Sexual impulses left on their own have nothing to do with the feelings, timing, or desires of the other person. However, mature lovers are able to tame their sexual impulses so that they serve the relationship, not just themselves. So if you have self-control, you allow your love and value for your spouse (not your passions) to control your sexual urges, "that each of you should learn to control his own body in a way that is holy and honorable" (1 Thessalonians 4:4).

Acceptance: Embracing Reality

Acceptance has to do with being able to relate lovingly and without judgment to everything about your mate. It is embracing the reality of his or her strengths and weaknesses, gifts, and imperfections. It does not mean that you approve of everything about your spouse, but it means you are willing to relate to all of him or her without condemnation, even those parts with which you don't agree or of which you don't approve. God in Christ offers us this kind of acceptance (Romans 15:7).

Sexuality requires you to be open and exposed, with all your blemishes and scars. Acceptance creates an environ-ment in which you and your spouse are aware of what the other lacks, but you don't allow those imperfections to stop the flow of love and gratitude for each other. You are so much in love with the character and soul of your beloved that accepting the body is a small thing. However, if you don't convey acceptance, or your partner does not feel acceptable regardless of what you say and do, then he or she will tend to hide, emotionally and sometimes physically.

Here's an example of what can happen. We know a couple in which the wife, after having two kids, had gotten out of shape. She was not obese, but she did not look or feel the way she wanted to. She felt very unat-tractive physically, and she was one of those people who tend to be self-critical. Her husband didn't help matters when he nagged her to get back in shape. His pestering joined with her self-condemnation, and she began to feel conditionally loved and under the law of perfection and guilt. As a result, she began to lose her sexual desire.

When they discovered what was going on, her husband rallied to her side. He let her know, "I am really sorry I've made you feel worse about your body. I want you to know that no matter what happens, I love you and I desire only you. Let me know if I put you under the law again, because I don't want you to feel that." His acceptance and grace helped her to feel more loved, and, in time, more sexual. In fact, she began to get back into a good diet and workout program too. Things went well for them after that, but it is important to note that these events happened only after she experienced acceptance from him.

One of the greatest gifts of marriage is that of sex. If you are experiencing difficulties in this wonderful area of life and don't know what to do about them, do not resign yourself to the problem. God has a way, through your growth in him, your marriage, and his resources. Ask him for the next step.